**For Anna and Lucas**

Our hopes for you children
Quite simply, are these:
That you always say "thank you,"
"you're welcome" and "please."
May your hearts remain full
of laughter and love
And thanks for the blessings
that come from above.

*Jodi Holley Cope*

2004

# South Dakota

## An Alphabetical Scrapbook

Written and Designed by **JODI HOLLEY LATZA**

Photographed by **GREG LATZA**

Bounding across the grassy hills
For an **ANTELOPE**
doesn't take long.
So you have to watch closely —
hey, look over there!
No wait ... it's already gone.

A a

Pronghorn antelope, the fastest animal in the western hemisphere, can run as fast as 60 miles per hour.

With thick, woolly coats
they're really quite hairy.
**BISON** live in a herd
and graze on the prairie.

# B b

As recently as the mid-1800s, millions of bison, also known as buffalo, roamed the Great Plains.

Not home for a king, but a "kernel" instead,
It's the only **CORN PALACE** we've found.
With walls adorned in colorful grain
It's the largest bird feeder around.

Mitchell Corn Palace designers use 11 shades of corn, as well as rye, milo, sourdock and brome grass to make new murals each year.

**DAMS** help control the "Big Muddy's" flow,
Making sure the Missouri stays where it should go.
The rushing water, with all its might
Helps power plants generate heat and light.

Dams along the Missouri River in South Dakota include Oahe, Big Bend, Fort Randall and Gavins Point, from north to south.

# Ee

No monster, meteorite
or major explosion,
But the natural
phenomenon known as
**EROSION**
Created the rough,
unforgiving shape
Of the Badlands' unique
and scenic landscape.

After taking 65 million years to accumulate their flat layers, the South Dakota Badlands are eroding an average of one inch per year.

# Ff

**FOSSILS** tell a fantastic story
About dinosaurs during their days of glory.
Many a T-Rex met its fate
In the western part of this great state!

"Sue" and "Stan," the two most complete Tyrannosaurus rex skeletons ever found, were discovered in South Dakota.

# Gg

Rippling with the slightest breeze
And fresh-smelling after the rain,
Plentiful **GRASSLANDS**
once waved like an ocean
To greet pioneers on the plains.

Covered wagons settlers drove across the grassy plains were
called "prairie schooners" because the white canvas canopies
that covered them looked like the sails on a ship.

At **HARVEST** time,
when the crops
are brought in,
There's plenty of work
to be done.
But when the bin's full
and brimming with grain
Again there is time
for some fun!

# H h

It takes just nine seconds for a combine to harvest enough wheat to make about 70 loaves of bread.

Slippery, clear, shiny and hard;
Thin, frozen water can catch you off guard.
So before you set out to fish or to ski
Make sure the **ICE** is as thick as can be.

Ice must be *at least* four inches thick to support a person, five inches for a snowmobile and eight to 12 inches for a small vehicle.

For ropin' or ridin' — or most any chore
**JEANS** are the all-purpose gear
To keep your hide safe
from scratches and scrapes
But mostly to cover your rear!

Jj

Born of necessity in the 1850s during the California Gold Rush,
"waist overalls," now known as jeans, later became the preferred attire
for Black Hills miners and other laborers because of their durability.

Our world, seen through a **KID**'s curious eyes
Holds hopeful excitement and happy surprise.
Rancher or teacher, which path will *you* choose?
Just maybe you'll fit the governor's shoes!

The South Dakota capitol building in Pierre (pronounced "peer") was completed in 1910 at a cost of nearly one million dollars.

A favorite spot to drop in a line
The fish may not bite, but it's still a good time.
The **LAKE** is a great place to just get away
To get back to nature, to rest and to play.

L l

More than 120 lakes were formed in northeastern South Dakota by glaciers that moved through the area thousands of years ago.

Four great leaders, chiseled in stone
Look out from a tall mountainside.
**MOUNT RUSHMORE** stands
for the freedom we love
The cause for which soldiers have died.

The famous American presidents sculptor Gutzon Borglum carved
into Mount Rushmore are (left to right): George Washington,
the first president; Thomas Jefferson, the third president;
Theodore "Teddy" Roosevelt, the 26th president;
and Abraham Lincoln, the 16th president.

# N n

Dwarfing the trees on the Black Hills below
The **NEEDLES** point up to the sky.
Maybe giants could use them
for clothes they might sew,
But surely I don't want to try!

The 1,000 granite spires of the Needles in Custer State Park are believed to be about two *billion* years old.

Before there were bathrooms
and plumbing indoors
Using the potty
was often a chore.
When nature would call
through the door folks would go
On their way to the
**OUTHOUSE**
in rain, sleet or snow.

Though Gregory, S.D., boasts a museum dedicated to outhouses, the structures are still utilized by some rural churches and schools.

All through the winter
the **PASQUE** flower sleeps.
Waiting for springtime
a vigil it keeps
'Til the cold forest floor
thaws slightly, and then
The miracle happens
all over again.

# P p

The pasque flower, one of the earliest bloomers each spring and South Dakota's state flower, often erupts through the snow.

Thousands of minerals make up the earth
Still, it's hard to uncover
the few of great worth.
But value's not measured by money alone
Abundant rose **QUARTZ**
is our favorite stone.

One of the world's largest deposits of rose quartz, South Dakota's state mineral, is located near Custer in the Black Hills.

Cowboys and cowgirls
are put to the test
With riding and roping
Who's fastest? Who's best?
The crowd in the grandstand
will give a great roar
For the **RODEO** champion
who earns the best score.

R r

Traditional rodeos include seven timed events: saddle bronc riding,
bareback riding, barrel racing, calf roping, team roping,
steer wrestling and bull riding.

Ss

Some of the first who called this place home
The **SIOUX** have their own special tongue.
Preserving tradition through stories they tell
They keep culture alive for their young.

Siouan people are divided into three language groups: Lakota, Nakota and Dakota, names which all mean "friends."

# Tt

A portable tent made with buffalo hide,
The **TIPI** still stands as a symbol of pride
For the Sioux, who lived by their wits and their hands,
Following bison across prairie lands.

The tipi, also spelled "tepee" or "teepee," was traditionally constructed by women of the tribe.

Discover a whole different world **UNDERGROUND**,
Where stalactites, stalagmites and caverns abound.
Exciting, strange places so dark and so damp
To get a good view you must wear a head lamp.

Uu

Located in South Dakota's Black Hills, Jewel Cave and Wind Cave rank third and seventh longest in the world at 122 and 93 miles long.

# Vv

Ah, **VACATION**!
The day is all ours
To ride our bikes, swim
or sleep under the stars.
Relaxing together
out in the fresh air
Makes good memories
of time that we share.

Each year, nearly five million people, more than six times the population of South Dakota, visit its state parks.

**Ww**

Blowing across the flat, treeless plains
the **WIND** has a life all its own.
It can howl at your window
on dark, stormy nights
Or chill you right through
to the bone.

The strongest gusts of wind during a blizzard or thunderstorm can reach
100 miles per hour and can top 300 mph inside a tornado.

# X x

Imagine the things e**XPLORERS** once saw
When first setting foot on this land.
No roads, cars or fences, no houses or schools
Only beauty, still unspoiled by man.

South Dakota's earliest evidence of European explorers is a lead plate left in 1743 by the Verendrye brothers near Fort Pierre.

**YELLOW**'s the color
to chase gloom away,
Like sunflowers bright
on a hot summer day
or clover in bloom, a sunset held dear,
And the warm, friendly people
who welcome you here.

South Dakota is the nation's second-leading producer of sunflowers, which are harvested primarily for their oil.

# Zz

At **ZERO** degrees
in wintertime
It's best to spend
the day inside.
Enjoy some cocoa
by the fire
Until the temperature
climbs higher.

The lowest recorded temperature in South Dakota was a bone-chilling 58 degrees *below* zero (Fahrenheit) at McIntosh in 1936.

# Thanks and Acknowledgements

**A & B:** The antelope and bison cow and calves were photographed at Custer State Park.

**C:** The Mitchell High School "Kernels" play their home basketball games in the Corn Palace.

**D:** The Oahe Dam was photographed on the way back from shooting the photo for "H."

**E:** This adventurous couple chose to picnic on an outcropping along the Badlands Loop Road.

**F:** Blanche Huper was photographed with a Tyrannosaurus rex skull at the Black Hills Institute of Geological Research in Hill City.

**G:** This prairie scene was captured just north of Summit.

**H:** The combines pictured here are from the Judy and Wilbert Ohlmann farm near Midland.

**I:** This curious little girl was found peeking beneath the ice at the annual Wall Lake Ice Fishing Derby near Hartford.

**J:** Young cowboys wear their hats and jeans at the Fort Pierre Rodeo *every* July 4.

**K:** Speaking of young cowboys, our nephew Joseph Gran is the one in front of the Capitol in Pierre.

**L:** The canoeists in this scene are paddling on Lake Herman near Madison.

**M:** Morning is one of the best times to view Mount Rushmore, when the light changes the granite from brown to orange to yellow and finally, to white.

**N:** Breaks in the clouds highlighted these needles in the foreground of Cathedral Spires.

**O:** We knew the spelling should read "paradise," but this outhouse in Cottonwood was *too* perfect to pass up.

**P:** This pasque was photographed along the shores of Sheridan Lake in the Black Hills.

**Q:** Our daughter Anna was the model for this photograph. How could we do a book for kids without using one of our own?!

**R:** Again, the Fourth of July in Fort Pierre means great rodeo action!

**S & T:** Dancers swirl at the annual Flandreau powwow, and many Native American participants stay in tipis during the three-day event.

**U:** Fellow photographer Paul Horsted and caving expert Steve Baldwin (right) invited Greg on an exciting trek through a winding cave south of Pringle. Steve is shown collecting water samples from a stalactite.

**V:** This Black Hills campground is located east of Custer.

**W:** Grass sways under a windmill south of Beresford.

**X:** Ole Olsen keeps busy portraying French trader Pierre Dorion, a man who accompanied Lewis & Clark for part of their historic voyage. Olsen lives in Elk Point, near the spot where this photograph was taken, along the Missouri River.

**Y:** Greg had to stand on his tip-toes to reach the level of this particular sunflower.

**Z:** This set of coyote tracks was found just up the road from Greg's boyhood farm near Letcher.

Special thanks to John Maniaci for providing the spark! And finally, Jodi would like to thank Greg for all his hard work and constant encouragement during this project. She could not have done it without him! Dedicated to the memory of Emery and Jo Markwed, loving grandparents.

# South Dakota
# FACTS

On November 2, 1889, South Dakota became the 40th U.S. state, the same day as its neighbor, North Dakota.

South Dakota is 380 miles across and 210 miles, top to bottom. It is the 17th largest state, with a total area of 77,121 square miles.

**State Animal**
Coyote

**State Bird**
Chinese Ring-Necked Pheasant

**State Capitol**
Pierre

**State Dessert**
Kuchen

**State Drink**
Milk

**State Fish**
Walleye

**State Flower**
American Pasque

**State Fossil**
Triceratops

**State Grass**
Western Wheat Grass

**State Gemstone**
Fairburn Agate

**State Insect**
Honey Bee

**State Mineral Stone**
Rose Quartz

**State Motto**
Under God
the People
Rule

**State Musical Instrument**
Fiddle

**State Nickname**
The Mount Rushmore
State

**State Song**
"Hail South Dakota"

**State Tree**
Black Hills Spruce

# peopleScapes
## PUBLISHING

© 2000, 2002 by PeopleScapes, Inc.
Sioux Falls, South Dakota USA

Text © Jodi Holley Latza
Photographs © Greg Latza

Published by PeopleScapes, Inc.
P. O. Box 88821
Sioux Falls, SD 57109

www.peoplescapes.com

Produced and Published in the United States of America by PeopleScapes Inc.
Printed in the Republic of Korea by Doosan Printing.

Second Printing

Library of Congress Card Number: 00-191683

ISBN 0-9673485-2-8

Jodi Holley Latza and Greg Latza live in Sioux Falls, South Dakota, with their children, Anna and Luke.

Jodi is a freelance writer and graphic designer and Greg is a freelance photographer. They started PeopleScapes in 1997 and have published two other books to date, *Back on the Farm: Celebrating South Dakota Farm and Ranch Families* and *Hometown, S.D.: Life in Our Small Towns.*

*Alphabetical Scrapbook* began as an extension of the bedtime reading ritual that occurs nightly in the Latza home and the family's love for their state. The Latzas hope it helps to foster a tradition of literacy and family togetherness for its readers, whatever their ages.

Matt Kryger

A b C d e F g H i J k L m N o

P Q r s t U v W x y Z

Z y X w u T S R q p o n M l

K i l h G f E H D c B a

A b C d e F g i J k L m N o

P Q r s t U v W x y Z

W e L O v e A N n a & L U K E

K i l h G f E H D c B a

A b C d e F g i J k L m N c

P Q r s t U v W x y Z

Z y X w v T S R q p o n M l

K i l h G f E H D c B a